Chakras

A Self Help Manual For Reducing Anxiety And Boosting Positive Emotions

(Your Unique Road Map To Recovery And Mastery Of One Of Your Most Potent Astrological Energies)

Eulalio Cavazos

TABLE OF CONTENT

Meditation on a Subject That Is More Generic Regarding Visualisation...1

Simple Techniques to Balance the Solar Plexus Chakra 19

Common Misconceptions..24

The Sixth Chakra...37

Change your mindset...46

Play the observer..47

What the Opening of the Throat Chakra Feels Like...49

The Pituitary Gland..64

B. Influence of the Navatara on personality traits and life experiences 72

C. Interplay between the Navataras and other astrological factors 73

Sensual Rituals 79

3.2 Tools for Chakra Healing...................................96

The Second Chakra — Svadhisthana 105

The Third Chakra — Manipura 107

The Chakras and Physical Health 120

Chakra Healing for Physical Health 123

Meditation on a Subject That Is More Generic Regarding Visualisation

When it comes to the process of healing, visualisations pack a significant punch. What you picture in your head has a significant bearing on the spiritual health of the person who is imagining it. Therefore, if you are dealing with energy that has been stuck or obstructed, visualising a healthy flow of energy will assist you in unblocking your chakras.

Now that we've established that this is the objective, let's look at a straightforward meditation that can help you achieve it while also helping you to centre yourself and protect the revitalised energy you've created.

"Find a place where you won't be disturbed and where you may lie down or sit in comfort for this exercise in visualisation. To achieve a state of relaxation, give yourself a moment to pause, slow down, and focus on taking deep, calm breaths.

Visualise a crimson core that is alive and pulsating with light at the base of your spine to start. Sensitise this part of your body to the warmth and energy that is pulsating from it. This is the root chakra in your body. Imagine it twirling around freely while emitting a brilliant light. Permit this energy to offer you with a sense of protection and security while also helping to ground you to the Earth.

The next step is to repeat the previous method for each of the other chakras. This means that you should visualise the sacral chakra in your navel area, the solar plexus chakra positioned above your stomach, the heart chakra in the centre of your chest, the throat chakra at the base of your throat, the third eye chakra situated on your brow, and finally the crown chakra located above your head. Visualise their unique hues, and in your mind's eye, see their energy freely flowing without any obstructions. Take long, deep breaths as you let go of any energy that has become blocked. It is important to keep in mind that in addition to visualising, you have the option of repeating affirmations that have meaning for your soul.

After you have cleansed and visualised each chakra in turn, you should then direct your attention to the seven chakras as a collective entity. Imagine them revolving in a way that is both brilliant and in perfect harmony, as if they were generating a stunning symphony of pulsating energy inside of you. Take note of the pleasant sensations and the way in which your energy body is aligned. Spend a few minutes soaking in this experience and getting in tune with the energy that is already within you.

When you are ready, take a few calm, deep breaths, and then open your eyes slowly to bring your attention back to the here and now. Permit yourself to take this revitalised energy and sense of equilibrium with you as you go about the rest of your day.

It is important to keep in mind that although the procedures that have been outlined above are effective tools, chakra healing is a comprehensive process. Therefore, incorporating a variety of practises into your overall healing path (including, of course, some much-needed self-care) will be beneficial.

Let's find out now what the distinctive qualities of each chakra are, as well as how you can bring them into balance with the assistance of these many techniques, and most importantly, through shadow work.

How to Unblock Your Sacral Chakra

- Choose zesty essential oils like orange, jasmine, sage, and ylang-ylang to open up your sacral chakra. These are energizing, balancing, and will improve your self-esteem.

- Water is the element of the sacral chakra. Go for a refreshing swim, drink more water, and take long salted and fragranced baths with essential oil.

- Heal with crystals like tiger's eye, citrine, and tangerine quartz. Use them during meditation to draw on their energetic healing powers. Always keep your crystals cleansed and flowing with their unique frequency.

- Use yoga poses that open up the hip area as these will unblock your sacral chakra. The butterfly pose, advanced baby pose, and downward facing dog are some yoga poses that you can use to stretch these areas of your body and release tension and stress you may beholding on to in your sacral chakra center.

- Pay attention to your negative sentiments, thoughts, and feelings about your body, sexuality, and creative abilities, and start shifting those thoughts to more empowering and healing alternatives to bring your sacral chakra back in balance and alignment with your authenticity.

  - Embrace your authenticity, dance, and have more fun. Be freer with yourself, and get untangled from the negativity surrounding you. Put on your favorite music and your dancing shoes, and get those hips moving again and your chakra flowing (*Unblocking Your Sacral Chakra for Confidence & Creativity*, 2022).

CHAMBER 9: IMPARTIALITY

We are used to immediately analyzing, comparing, evaluating, and classifying everything we perceive. Our brain compares every external stimulus with similar experiences from our memory and classifies it into categories such as "pleasant" or "unpleasant."

On this basis, the actions that seem most appropriate for coping with the situation are initiated according to our existing response patterns. This process takes place, at least in part, unconsciously in our thalamus, the "gate of consciousness" of our brain.

Real mindfulness is only possible if we can detach ourselves from the conscious parts of this kind of evaluation, or at least slow it down a bit. Impartiality means above all the willingness to perceive everything that happens as if we were experiencing it for the first time. It means at least trying to put aside everything we think we know about the situations and people we encounter.

> *Impartiality means not immediately dismissing seemingly obvious or familiar things as habitual*

Think about the last time you traveled to someplace away from home for a vacation or some other reason. Immediately after returning from a long trip, you probably saw your everyday surroundings with slightly different eyes. Everything felt somehow "fresher", didn't it? Usually, this effect lasts only a few hours or days, and then we fall back into our daily routine.

Through meditation, we want to rediscover this feeling, this fresh way of perceiving, and integrate it as a state of mind into our everyday life. In Zen, this is called cultivating the beginner's mind.

So, impartiality means seeing, hearing, feeling, and thinking as impartially as possible. You could say it's trying to perceive from inspiration—from what's there in the moment—rather than from an expectation of how things should be—or how they will be.

You may also know people in your environment who often behave in ways that trigger negative reactions in you. Your boss, your family, your coworkers. Since this has probably happened many times in your life, you may consciously or unconsciously expect it to happen again the next time.

Your experiences in life are determined to a significant extent by your, often unquestioned, expectations

This expectation in itself increases the likelihood that the conflict will occur again—because you are unconsciously building resonances that can also "trigger" the people or situations that give you a triggering impulse.

Worse, this expectation increases the likelihood that you will react as you always do. By practicing the ability to look at things without bias, you are increasingly able to overcome your conditioning and respond spontaneously to old and new situations. This attitude is usually much more conducive to finding a solution that benefits everyone involved than acting out old patterns stored in your memory.

To summarize the results of this chamber: We can train our impartiality in everyday life by noticing our expectations, then admitting that things might be different this time, and finally focusing on being as mindful as possible about what is happening.

When we practice mindfulness regularly, we almost automatically find it easier to look at things more calmly and without bias. We can further support this process by setting a conscious intention to be more mindful in our daily lives. There is also an active meditation that can help this process happen more and more spontaneously within us. This will be our exercise for this chamber.

The Fourth Chakra - Anahata Chakra

The heart chakra location is usually opposite the centerline running between the nipples. Still, sometimes it is moved slightly to the right of the sternum, although not directly above the heart. It is associated with the conquest of air, nature, and nada, the sound of cosmic consciousness. By meditating on this center, you can feel how the energy flows throughout the entire nervous system as if it is filled with magnetism. Many traditions of spiritual development emphasize the importance of the heart chakra as the chakra that needs to be awakened in the first place to experience a spiritual awakening since it is here that the energies of the lower and upper levels of consciousness merge, which symbolize two intersecting triangles. In addition, Anahata, combining the powers of different chakras, also connects the left and right sides of the body, yin and yang qualities.

Isha is the God of this chakra; he sits on a black antelope or gazelle, which symbolizes speed and ease of air. Isha is the supreme God, endowed with full yogic power, omniscient, and omnipresent. It is white and symbolizes purity; it has three eyes; the third represents knowledge of samadhi. When its form arises during meditation, fears disappear, and concentration intensifies.

The yantra images of the heart chakra include intersecting triangles, inside which are a bright golden creature and Kakini Shakti, the lightning-colored goddess who radiates light and joy. Kakini is called the keeper of Anahata's doors and meditates on it; a person learns to stabilize prana and remove obstacles on the way to Isha. When the goddess is red, her power controls pranic energy; she is white and is Isha's consciousness.

The twelve scarlet petals associated with Anahata represent waiting, excitement, diligence, affection, hypocrisy, weakness, selfishness, separation, greed, fraud, indecision, and regret. Meditation on this chakra brings possession of sound. If you say the mul mantra during meditation, you are more prepared to understand God, as a person gains control over his feelings, mainly by reducing the sense of touch. Then, as they say, not a single desire will remain unfulfilled - a person will forever plunge into a state of bliss.

Suppose you look from a different point of view. In that case, we can assume that freed from attachment to all "heart" desires (as evidenced by the qualities embodied in the petals), a person gains the ability to distract the senses from all worldly things and thus acquire a state of bliss first for short periods and then forever.

The qualities of compassion, acceptance, and unconditional love are signs of the balanced functioning of this chakra. Indifference, passivity, and sadness are signs of an imbalance — some authors associate arthritis and respiratory problems with cardiac chakra, cardiovascular disease, and hypertension.

The opening of this chakra is considered feasible with the help of the skin; that is, you need to surpass the sense of touch, which is done by achieving control over sensory perception through kumbhaka (breath-holding). A common way to discover the energy of Anahata is a meditation on it with the simultaneous presentation of light or breathing in and breathing out air from it.

Simple Techniques to Balance the Solar Plexus Chakra

Once again, we will start with the yoga poses. The reason I love yoga so much is that as I sit here at my desk for a few hours I start to feel a bit sluggish. All it takes is for me to stand up and do a couple of poses to stretch out my body and feel the rush of blood, and energy to parts that have me still for too long. Give it a try!

Cobra Pose (Bhujangasana)

1. Lie down on your stomach, with your legs extended behind you and your toes flat on the floor. Place your hands on the floor, palms down, next to your shoulders.

2. Inhale and slowly lift your head, chest, and shoulders off the ground, keeping your elbows close to your body. Your hands should still be on the floor, supporting your upper body.
3. Hold the pose for a few breaths, while keeping your gaze forward and your shoulders relaxed. Do not strain your neck or push yourself too far.
4. To release the pose, exhale and lower your upper body back down to the ground, relaxing your arms and shoulders.

Reverse Plank (Puvottanasana)

1. Begin by sitting on the floor with your legs extended in

front of you, feet flexed and palms resting on the ground behind you, fingers pointing towards your feet.
2. Press your palms and feet firmly into the ground and lift your hips off the ground. Your body should be in a straight line from your head, through your spine, to your heels.
3. Keep your arms straight and engaged, shoulders down and away from your ears, and chest lifted. Keep your gaze straight ahead.
4. Hold the pose for a few breaths, gradually increasing the duration with practice.
5. To release the pose, slowly lower your hips back down to the ground and rest.

Boat Pose (Navasana)

1. Sit on the mat with your legs extended in front of you and your hands resting on the ground beside your hips.
2. Lean back slightly and lift your feet off the ground, keeping your knees bent.
3. Slowly straighten your legs, so your body forms a V-shape. Keep your chest lifted, and your shoulders relaxed.
4. Extend your arms forward alongside your legs, keeping them parallel to the floor. If possible, straighten your legs fully, but do not strain.
5. Hold the pose for a few breaths, engaging your core muscles and maintaining your balance.
6. To release the pose, exhale and lower your feet and hands back to the ground.

Common Misconceptions

Even the most open of minds are not immune to preconceived notions or cultural biases sneaking into their first impression of something. Especially for a concept that has gone through so many iterations and has been rebranded so many times, it can be hard to pinpoint exactly what chakra healing is. To begin this journey on equal footing, let's debunk some of the common myths about chakras.

> 1. Energy is produced in the chakras, which is why our energy is low with a blocked chakra.

Contrary to popular belief, chakras do not generate energy for us out of thin air. Rather, they are the terminals in which our natural life force and the universe's energy can gather and be exchanged.

When a chakra is blocked or overtaken by stagnant energy, this vital essence struggles to flow through the body. This creates energy imbalances, as well as disrupts communication between the chakras themselves. Any unbalanced level of energy can cause a blockage, not just low energy.

2. Chakras belong to a specific religion.

All of us have the chakra system within our bodies. While it does come from a religious text and is a spiritual pillar of Hinduism and Buddhism, it is at its core something that anyone can harness during their spiritual journey.

Considering the infinite system variations and theories that have been proposed over the centuries, the current seven-chakra system as we know it is the perfect culmination of Eastern and Western ideology. As long as we are respectful of its roots, are willing to listen to Hindu or Buddhist practitioners, and recognize the validity of other chakra systems, we can keep this streak of collaborative wisdom going for decades to come!

3. Chakras are demonic in nature.

Likely due to Leadbeater's use of words like "serpent's fire" and "satanic" in his book, some might assume chakras are demonic. Yes, chakras have been explored in an esoteric context, but, as we've learned during our extensive history lesson, chakras started off as a form of meditation and visualization in Hindu rituals.

The point of chakra meditation is to access our life force energy. We explore these channels of energy not to do evil, but rather to connect to the earth and find equilibrium within ourselves. If anything, looking into our chakras is a sign that we want to better ourselves as people.

4. You can focus solely on one chakra.

While you can certainly target specific chakras that feel especially blocked, it is important to keep all chakras within the system in sync. If one is out of order, it disrupts the entire flow of life force throughout the rest of the body. Do what you can to remove that one chakra's blockage, but be aware that neglecting the other chakras will likely perpetuate the weakness of your energy's flow.

> 5. You cannot (or do not need to) do the work yourself, because chakra healing has to be done by a professional healer.

Self-help starts and ends with *you*, and chakra healing is no different. Visiting a professional isn't necessary. All forms of holistic healing require effort on your behalf, even when it's hard. Visiting a professional isn't mandatory to see real change happening in your life. It is possible to be your own healer!

That being said, if you feel stuck or want expert advice, professional healers can certainly work wonders for you. Sometimes being your own healer means admitting when you need help. You may be leading your journey but you don't have to walk this path alone.

> 6. We take on life force energy from other people.

Have you felt drained after spending time with someone? It may feel like they are energy vampires who have sucked all the energy out of you. Their negative energy is definitely influencing your own, but they are not actually taking life force energy from your body.

Or sometimes, when consoling someone else, you might feel like you've absorbed their negative emotions. This is more likely to do with empathy. Our actual vibrational frequency may change in response to the situation, but we cannot actually steal negative energy from their chakras unless we are actively doing energy work on them.

The shift in our emotions or energy level is likely because humans are social creatures who often form connections through mirroring. To help that person feel seen and understood, we might involuntarily mirror their emotional expression or relive our own experiences that are similar (which may dampen our mood). We hope our empathy and care can help them to sort out their own energetic imbalances, but we are not removing their negative energy or absorbing it into our own body.

7. Balancing your chakras will cure any and all of your ailments,

including physical or emotional concerns.

Aligned chakras do not guarantee emotional balance, nor do they cancel out health issues in that chakra's correlated area. Holistic healing is never a replacement for seeing a physician or therapist, but is rather something to add to your wellness regimen.

While a lot of the entries in this book will mention physical ailments and mental conditions that are considered a sign of chakra imbalance, this is not to claim that the openness of our chakras dictate our health. These ailments are not caused by blocked chakras, nor will they disappear upon your chakra being opened. Rather, their inclusion is to show how blocked chakras can manifest in the body, or that pains in the body can aggravate an already blocked chakra. A healthy chakra system simply means that our life force energy is flowing nicely.

Chapter 2: Creativity & the Sacral Chakra

Guided Meditation #3

Step 1

The sacral chakra is the body's natural hub for creativity, whether it's expressed artistically, physically, or in terms of literal reproduction. If you've been feeling lack of inspiration or creative direction in life, focus on what you want to manifest to change that. For just a moment before you close your eyes, think of what you'd like to draw into your life or what you'd like to create.

Step 2

Now that you have this vision in your mind, come to a comfortable seated or reclined position and allow your eyes to close. Find your creative center. Breathe deeply and exhale your full breath a few times in succession. Get out all that old, stagnant air that's been keeping you held back. Breathe forcefully all that yuck out, making way for the new, for inspiration, and for the possibility of future creation. Bring your hands to that space a few inches below your navel that's ruled by your sacral chakra and try to breathe all the way down into it.

Creativity in the Present Moment

Step 3

In order to boost that creative center, even with all your breath flowing into it, you'll have to do a little introspection. Think of what could be blocking this chakra for you. What's been holding you back, artistically or physically? Are there doubts or voices keeping you in a place of doubt? If fertility and childbirth is your version of creation, have there been health problems that can cause issues for reproduction? Are there symptoms of future health issues in the making in this space of your body? What can you discern from looking deeply?

Step 4

In this present moment, as you breathe deeply and find root in the earth, imagine your creativity as a thing in and of itself. This thing could be just a blob, undefined and grey. It could be that vision of what you want to create or of what you wanted to attract into your life. It could be your creativity given an animal form for the moment. However you picture your creativity, just do so, and try to keep breathing into that same sacral chakra space of your body while you do this.

Step 5

As you conjure this image of your creativity personified, how are you feeling? Is there a thought the keeps crossing your mind? Try not to block out these voices and sensations, for they are absolutely essential as we strive to clear this chakra for good. If you hear voices or doubts, what are they telling you? The biggest question is this: are they trying to keep you from creating due to a state of **fear**? If your answer is even a semi-questioning "yes," it's a spiritual "yes."

The Sixth Chakra

Welcome to this beautiful third-eye chakra meditation. Allow me to guide you to unlock and balance the sixth Chakra, the one that connects you to inner knowing. It is the center of visualization where you create and manifest the reality of your desire. Find yourself in a spot where you can easily ignore the outside world. Making sure you are in a comfortable position. Take a nice slow breath in and exhale, relaxing. You may close your eyes at any time when you balance the chakras by meditating on them, concentrating all of your focus on each individually. You begin to see the events in your life as symbolic, with beautiful lessons to be learned. Take a nice breath in and let it go. Allow each breath to relax you. Breathing in and out.In and out. Now bring your focus to the third eye chakra found in the center of your forehead, just slightly above the eyebrows. Bring all of your focus between your eyebrows, and when your concentration gets interrupted, simply return your awareness to this location. As often as you find yourself straying, see how it glows in a deep indigo color, A perfect mix of blue and purple.

You can visualize cis Chakra along with a symbol of an inverted perfect triangle. The indigo color radiates out from your third eye. The triangle is perfectly placed there. Now feel how you can spin this chara just by imagining it. See it accelerating until it is spinning so fast that the indigo is glowing faster than the speed of light. Repeat this mantra five times. Free the mind. Free the mind. Free the mind. Free the mind. Free the mind. Take a deep breath and feel the power of oxygen. Expanding the third eye chakra until it is radiating out far from your body. Feel the deep expansion of inner knowledge happening to you right now. How would you describe the feeling of the third eye chakra? It opens the center of your forehead, allowing access for the spirit from the ether to make its way into your mind. The power of spirituality is affecting every aspect of your mind, freeing you from fear, doubt, and suffering. You can see the third eye chakra fully open and free, spinning brightly with influential indigo. Good. Take a deep breath in, and as you inhale, imagine that you are pulling in the energy from the infinite source of knowledge.

Connecting to the universal mind.Right between your eyebrows. Wisdom is pouring through your entire body, illuminating the other chakras along the way with the power of inner knowledge, giving them the energy to open and move freely. You hear the words; I have eternal wisdom. The third eye chakra is now completely open and ready to connect you with all there is to understand. Feeling a compassionate nature returning to you, visualizing the end to all suffering. Breathe in again deeply and fully. And one last time, breathe in and out. Wonderful. Gently begin to return your awareness to your current surroundings. Open your eyes and see the world around you as yours to explore the endless knowledge it has to offer.

Mediation to heal and balance the Solar Plexus Chakra:

Find a quiet and comfortable space where you can sit or lie down in a relaxed position. Close your eyes and take a few deep breaths, allowing your body and mind to settle.

Bring your attention to the area of your upper abdomen, where the Solar Plexus Chakra is located. Visualize a radiant, glowing yellow light in this area, pulsating with energy and vitality.

As you breathe deeply, imagine this yellow light expanding and growing brighter with each breath. Feel its warmth spreading throughout your entire abdominal region, enveloping your Solar Plexus Chakra.

Now, focus on your breath, inhaling deeply and exhaling fully. With each inhale, imagine that you are drawing in pure, vibrant energy into your Solar Plexus Chakra. Visualize this energy as a bright yellow light, filling your entire being with confidence, personal power, and inner strength.

As you exhale, release any stagnant or blocked energy from your Solar Plexus Chakra. Visualize this energy as a dark smoke or heavy weight leaving your body, carrying away any doubts, fears, or feelings of powerlessness.

With each breath, feel the radiant yellow light of the Solar Plexus Chakra growing stronger and more vibrant. Sense a deep sense of empowerment and confidence arising within you. Allow this energy to flow freely, filling you with a sense of inner strength and personal power.

Now, bring to mind a situation or challenge in your life where you desire to assert yourself and embrace your personal power. Visualize yourself handling this situation with confidence, grace, and assertiveness. See yourself standing tall, speaking your truth, and taking decisive action in alignment with your authentic self.

As you hold this visualization, feel the energy of the Solar Plexus Chakra intensifying. Sense the power and strength radiating from within you. Know that you have the inner resources and personal power to overcome any obstacles or challenges that come your way.

Stay in this state of meditation for as long as feels comfortable, continuing to breathe deeply and allowing the energy of the Solar Plexus Chakra to expand and empower you.

When you're ready to conclude the meditation, take a few final deep breaths, gradually bringing your awareness back to your physical surroundings. Open your eyes and take a moment to reflect on the experience.

Carry the energy and insights from this meditation with you throughout your day, embracing your personal power, cultivating self-confidence, and taking inspired action in alignment with your true self.

Remember that regular practice of this meditation can contribute to the healing and balancing of your Solar Plexus Chakra, fostering a greater sense of empowerment, self-esteem, and inner strength. Embrace your personal power, honor your worth, and allow the radiant energy of the Solar Plexus Chakra to guide you towards a life of confidence, assertiveness, and authentic self-expression.

Change your mindset

There are a few unintentional roadblocks that tend to come up for many kundalini practitioners. Mainly, you'll want to perform a couple of checks to ensure that your mindset is as aligned with the kundalini awakening as possible. Reject as many sources of negativity in your life as you can. If you can't get rid of them, try to face them and call them out, or you could just outright ignore them. On a personal level, too, you can work to change negativity into its opposite extreme of expression when it comes to your personality traits, routines, habits, and more. Furthermore, the less attachment you have to material things and patterns, the more open you become to the changes awakening has in store for you. Overall, therefore, reject (and possibly counteract) negativity and attachment, and you will surely flourish. (As a general note, if this method doesn't work for you, don't force yourself to attempt it, especially if it creates toxic effects for you. In that case, you may have a blockage of the third eye or crown chakra that needs to be worked through before full awakening can be achieved.)

Play the observer

Do you often find yourself as the center of attention, in more than just a team-sport-member or theatre-troupe-member way? Do you generally crave that type of support and public awareness? Now comes the trickier part. When you *are* the center of attention, do you notice things better or worse? Do you take in the whole picture or do you get tunnel vision for only what you're doing (and perhaps what the viewer takes in)? I'd be willing to venture a guess that you *aren't* fully aware of what's going on, particularly in your surroundings, at times when you fill that public position. Maybe a little more time spent playing the observer instead would help you. For people who resonate with the message behind this point, try to be a little more subtle in public settings. See who rises instead and then just listen to what they have to say. Interrupt your needs and urges in this way, and your kundalini will realize what a powerful energetic shift you're instigating, responding to its way in kind.

What the Opening of the Throat Chakra Feels Like

Since it takes time for the air to clear your throat chakra, the opening signs of this energetic center usually appear only gradually. Each person has different symptoms when rebalancing your chakras, and your experience may reflect the causes of the blockage and the approach you take for healing. As the energy starts to flow more freely through your throat chakra, you may notice the following:

- Throat Starts to Clear Up: If you previously had a chronic sore throat or issues with your vocal cords, you may notice them slowly starting to disappear. They may return occasionally but eventually will go away completely.

- Infections: Even if you haven't had mouth or gum diseases before, these may appear as your throat chakra is activated. As you continue the process, the infections will clear up.
- Asthma Flare-Ups: Asthma is a chronic condition whose symptoms often deteriorate before they start disappearing because the air traveling through your lungs aggravates the affected tissue. As your health improves, your body learns to combat this condition, and the flare-up will cease to appear.
- Fluctuating Thyroid Functions: As one of the most affected organs in a Vishuddha imbalance, your thyroid needs more time to heal, reflecting on your overall health. This gland produces

several essential hormones that keep your body and mind healthy. The functions of everything these hormones control will fluctuate, from your heartbeat and muscle strength to your metabolism.

- You Find It Easier to Communicate: One of the most indicative signs of a healthier Vishuddha is the improved ability to communicate with those around you. Actively honing your communication skills will facilitate the clearing process even more.
- Improved Listening Skills: As the air cleanses your throat chakra, it makes you more aware of your environment. This allows you to truly listen and comprehend what others

are telling you, no matter how subtly they go about it.

- Speaking the Truth: The more you listen to others, the more you'll notice them wanting to hear your opinions. It may come hard at first, but eventually, you'll learn how to speak your truth without hesitation or fear.
- Leaving Out Empty Words: This goes hand in hand with speaking the truth. You only say what you truly mean because it comes from within. You'll even find it more enjoyable to speak when your thoughts and speech become aligned.
- Alignment of Your Mind and Heart: In the beginning, you may find it challenging to balance what your logical mind dictates and

what your heart wishes. By balancing the throat chakra, these two sides will start to work in tandem.

- Finding Your Creativity: Freedom of speech isn't the only outlet you'll discover for your thoughts and emotions. Whether it's painting, music, or any other art or craft, you'll find many creative ways to express yourself.
- Improved Manifestation Skills: Learning to communicate with people will also teach you how to manifest your desires clearly through setting goals and productivity.
- The Pleasure of Being Heard: Transparent communication has even more beneficial outcomes. When you see others listen and validate your

opinions, this fills you with immeasurable satisfaction.
- Varying Discomfort Levels: At first, all these changes may heighten your distress, causing the flare-up of your symptoms. As Vishuddha starts clearing up, your discomfort slowly abates.
- Raised Self-Confidence: Feeling healthier and happier and communicating clearly and concisely can give your confidence an enormous boost. Making even the most dreaded decisions will become easier as you feel you can achieve whatever you set your mind to.

The Importance of Chakras in the Body

So, now that you know how connected the chakras really are, you can begin to see how a blockage in any of your chakras can really affect your ability to function. One chakra being blocked does not just mean that the certain aspect of your life controlled by that chakra is blocked but also that energy cannot freely flow throughout your whole system. You can think of this like a drain being blocked. Water can flow above and below the block but not through it, so your drain is unusable simply because one small part of it is not functioning properly. For a more complex analogy, we can turn back to our seven-floor office building. Let's say floor five is the communications department, representing the throat chakra. If this department stops working properly, the other departments might not be affected right away as they are still going about their business. But slowly, the company's relationships with other firms will deteriorate, beginning to erode their capacity for outreach. They will lose advertisements, which will lead to fewer new clients, and eventually reduced profits. They will also not be able to respond to customer complaints, which might lead to losing even repeat customers who were previously loyal. All of these repercussions will eventually lead to cuts in other departments, and if not fixed, a complete shutdown of the company. As you can see, just removing one essential aspect of the function of the company can lead to a massive restructuring and possibly even bankruptcy.

Let's map this back onto a human being and their chakra identity. If you have a blockage in your throat chakra, you might struggle with communication, be dishonest, or have social anxiety. These kinds of things won't necessarily directly affect your other chakras and their functions, since they will be operating on different wavelengths. However, over time, the struggles you are facing because of your throat chakra block will eventually come to affect the other facets of your life. Struggling with communication can ruin relationships, which touches your heart chakra. Being dishonest hurts your social reputation, which can affect your self-esteem and relationships. Having social anxiety can mean you withdraw from the world, even your friends and family, which disrupts your sense of home and self, affecting your root chakra. All of these reverberations will eventually block your ability to flow energy up to your crown chakra and truly have foresight in the world. What you will be left with is a mind preoccupied with the petty issues of the everyday and the inability to truly seek enlightened thought.

Choosing an Exercise That Works Best for You

You have a wide range of options.

If your area is prone to extreme weather, opt for an exercise program you can do indoors.

Choose an exercise activity you enjoy. Don't force yourself to do something simply because you think it is good for you.

Think about your budget when choosing an exercise routine. If you have limited resources, basketball or cycling may be a better option than sailing or skiing.

Take your fitness level and health into account. Don't pick a program that is too difficult for you. Be realistic. Opt for something you can do, especially if you are new to exercise. Start simple. Tweak your program as you work your way up.

One study published in 1987 in the Journal of Consulting and Clinical Psychology looked at 40 different women who were depressed. The women were split into two separate groups and told to either run or lift weights four times a week for eight weeks. Another study published more recently, in 2004 in The Primary Care Companion to The Journal of Clinical Psychiatry, looked at 90 depressed patients. They were also split into two groups. One group performed aerobic exercises like jogging or brisk walking and the other group performed non-aerobic exercises like weight training and stretching. Both groups were assigned the activities three times a week, 60 minutes at a time for eight weeks.

In both studies, no difference was found in the effectiveness of aerobic versus non-aerobic exercises in reducing the symptoms of depression. This is great news because it allows you to choose an exercise that fits your body type and personal interests.

There are a few theories on what might cause exercise to reduce depression, stress, and anxiety. They include the idea that increasing the body's core temperature can affect the brain in a way that causes relaxation afterward, that endorphins are released and cause you to feel good, that exercise can distract and help us reset our thought patterns, and that achieving goals through exercise helps us look at ourselves in a better light. With these in mind, you should ask yourself some questions about your workouts to determine if they are effective in reducing your depression. Ask yourself the following questions:

•Am I exercising vigorously enough to raise my body temperature?

•Do I feel good both during and after I exercise?

•Is my exercise demanding enough to distract me from negative thoughts?

•Am I reaching the exercise goals I have set for myself?

These questions can be a good guide to decide if your exercise program is being effective enough to reduce your depression and stress. Keep in mind that it is only a guide though. Many people, for example, find relief from depression by doing simple stretches for their exercise on some days. This does not raise the body's core temperature and is not very demanding. It can be meditative, though, which helps some people. The more you exercise the better idea you will have of what works and what doesn't.

Ultimately, the most important thing is that you just choose to exercise without stressing too much about how you do it. So, whether you run, hike, lift weights, swim, do yoga, or cycle you will be working toward improving your mental and physical health every time you do it.

Ancient Wisdom Related to the Pineal Gland

Many ancient spiritual traditions have referred to the pineal gland as the third eye. For some, this is because the pineal gland is located close to the visual cortex and is directly related to the interplay of light and darkness. Also, philosophers have believed that the pineal gland helps not only with physical but also spiritual vision—helping us "see" internal images more clearly.

Over the years, it has been called "the seat of the soul." In 2000, clinical psychiatrist Rick Strassman wrote about a possible effect of the pineal gland on our physical, mental, and spiritual health. In his book *DMT: The Spirit Molecule*, he talked at length about the pineal gland and its ability to secrete dimethyltryptamine (DMT), which is a strong psychoactive compound usually found in certain plants and animals. Since it is psychoactive in nature, it usually causes hallucinatory effects in people who consume it. According to

Strassman, the pineal gland can secrete this compound on its own, especially during major events such as birth and death. In this way, it can be instrumental in enhancing our life force as part of a spiritual awakening. It's important to note here that we have yet to find conclusive scientific evidence when it comes to a significant presence of DMT in our pineal gland.

However, a review was conducted to understand how the relationship between light, third eye, and the pineal gland can affect our physical and mental health. The review concluded that the pineal gland is much more complex than initially thought, and it has an effect not only on the secretion of important hormones like melatonin and serotonin, but also on DMT. This way, it seems to have an impact on various neurological and psychiatric conditions as well (Gheban et al., 2019).

The significance of the pineal gland is also present in

chronomedicine. Chronomedicine is derived from an understanding of how circadian rhythms work and how diseases develop due to the disruption of these cycles. According to the alternative medicine system of Ayurveda, our bodies and minds are regulated by three *doshas* (the sources of problems)—*vata*, *pitta*, and *kapha*. Since our doshas are intricately linked with our circadian rhythms, the pineal gland plays an important role in chronomedicine. Not only that, but the timing of our medicines is also dependent on these circadian rhythms (Kumar et al., 2018).

The Pituitary Gland

The pituitary gland is also pea-shaped and is seen as being physically closer to the location of the third eye. This is an important gland because it's instrumental in the secretion of most major hormones. Since it plays such a vital role in regulating our hormones and in creating balance within the body, it plays an important role in aligning our third eye chakra.

To understand the importance of the pituitary gland and hypothalamus in terms of the third eye chakra, we can look at children. You might have noticed that the heads of children need special protection. In fact, certain areas of their heads are extremely tender, and these areas are where the pituitary gland and hypothalamus reside. When you're holding an infant, for example, you might be advised to gently hold the tender part of their head for protection.

Now, we know that children are extremely intuitive by nature. They seem to have a natural curiosity not only for the physical world but also for the world that we don't perceive easily. In fact, their questions might give you an idea about their capacity to wonder about anything and everything at the same time. It's believed that this happens because their third eye is aligned at the time. Their consciousness is also raised and they are more susceptible to energies that adults cannot usually pick up. One theory which explains this is related to the different kinds of waves that our brain emits.

For example, when we feel sad, anxious, or angry, our brains emit *beta* waves. When we feel happy and calm, on the other hand, our brains emit *alpha* waves. It's said that infants and young children emit a higher number of alpha waves because their pituitary and hypothalamus region is tender. As we grow older and this region becomes less tender, the number of alpha waves emitted by our brains decrease, thus blocking our intuitive abilities.

The third kind of wave is known as *gamma* wave, which can only be experienced by people who meditate for long periods of time and reach a state of *samadhi*. During *samadhi*, the practitioner experiences complete ego dissolution. In other words, there's no difference between the person's individual consciousness and the Universal Consciousness. In some cases, samadhi might even lead to the person leaving their physical body for good.

These three waves are primarily responsible for the different states we experience in our daily lives as well as during our spiritual awakening process. In order to sharpen our intuition, we need to intensify the emission of alpha waves in our brain.

Chapter 4

Symptoms of an Imbalanced Throat Chakra

The throat chakra is the fifth chakra, located at the base of the neck, and is associated with our ability to communicate effectively and express ourselves authentically. When the throat chakra is imbalanced, we may experience a range of physical, emotional, and spiritual symptoms that can impact our overall well-being. In this article, we will explore some of the common symptoms of an imbalanced throat chakra, and how we can work to restore balance and harmony to this important energy center.

Physical Symptoms

One of the most common physical symptoms of an imbalanced throat chakra is a sore throat or other throat-related issues, such as hoarseness, difficulty swallowing, or chronic coughing. Other physical symptoms may include neck and shoulder pain, thyroid issues, or ear and sinus problems.

Emotional Symptoms

When the throat chakra is imbalanced, we may also experience a range of emotional symptoms, such as difficulty expressing ourselves, feeling unheard or misunderstood, or struggling to communicate effectively with others. We may also feel a sense of anxiety or fear around speaking our truth, or have a tendency to be overly critical or judgmental of ourselves or others.

Spiritual Symptoms

On a spiritual level, an imbalanced throat chakra can leave us feeling disconnected from our higher selves, and struggling to connect with our inner wisdom and guidance. We may also experience a lack of purpose or direction in our lives, or feel as though we are unable to fully express our true selves.

Restoring Balance to the Throat Chakra

If you are experiencing symptoms of an imbalanced throat chakra, there are many things you can do to restore balance and harmony to this important energy center. One of the most effective ways to balance the throat chakra is through meditation and visualization, which can help to clear any blockages or negative energy that may be present.

Another helpful practice is to engage in activities that support self-expression and creativity, such as writing, art, or music. By giving ourselves permission to express ourselves freely and authentically, we can begin to unlock the power of our throat chakra and cultivate a greater sense of inner peace and well-being.

In addition to these practices, it is also important to pay attention to our physical needs, and to take care of our bodies in a holistic way. This may involve eating a healthy diet, getting regular exercise, and engaging in practices such as yoga or tai chi that help to support overall physical and emotional well-being.

Ultimately, by taking steps to restore balance and harmony to the throat chakra, we can unlock our full potential for self-expression, communication, and spiritual growth. By connecting with our true selves and expressing ourselves authentically, we can cultivate a greater sense of purpose, direction, and fulfillment in our live

B. Influence of the Navatara on personality traits and life experiences

The Navatara that dominates a person's birth chart exerts a significant influence on their personality traits and life experiences. It shapes their approach to various aspects of life, including career, relationships, spirituality, and personal growth.

For example, someone born under the influence of the SampatNavatara may possess a natural affinity for material success and wealth accumulation. They are driven to achieve financial security and may excel in business or investment ventures. Their life experiences may revolve around abundance, prosperity, and the acquisition of material possessions.

On the other hand, an individual born under the VipatNavatara may face more challenges and obstacles in their life journey. These challenges contribute to their personal growth and resilience. They learn valuable lessons through adversity, which shapes their character and strengthens their ability to overcome obstacles.

C. Interplay between the Navataras and other astrological factors

The interplay between the Navataras and other astrological factors, such as planetary positions, aspects, and transits, adds depth and complexity to the interpretation of a birth chart.

For instance, the placement of planets within specific Navataras can modify or enhance the characteristics associated with that Navatara. The aspects between planets and the dominant Navatara can provide further insights into the dynamics of the individual's life experiences.

The interplay between the Navataras and other astrological factors is a crucial aspect of chart interpretation. It allows astrologers to provide a comprehensive analysis of an individual's unique personality, life path, and potentials. By considering the interactions between the Navataras and other astrological factors, astrologers can offer valuable guidance and support tailored to the individual's specific astrological makeup.

Feel the subtle flow of thoughts. Don't be surprised if you feel burdened by your thoughts. This is natural. All of us experience lethargy and sluggishness.

(Pause for 20 seconds)

Now, imagine a red dot at the Muladhara chakra. Observe the dot expanding slowly and graciously. It is now like a red ball. Let the red color expand more and more. Feel the Muladhara chakra bathed in a soft red glow. Remain in this state for a few seconds.

(Pause for 10 seconds)

Your Muladhara chakra is now getting healed. Do not expect magical results. You will have to practice this healing exercise for many days, even weeks to heal completely. This process is gradual. But the results are transformational. You will feel fully awakened and aware once the Muladhara chakra is healed.

Now, allow your consciousness to travel upward to the second chakra, which is located behind the sex organs. Sex is a potent force, which has the power to unleash your creativity.

The Swadishthana chakra is represented as water or effortless flow of energy. Like the flow of water, this energy will dissipate and drain away if it is not properly channelized.

Bring your thoughts of sex to the forefront of your mind. Do not hesitate. Do not shy away from your true feelings. Thoughts about sex are natural. Do not suppress your sexual fantasies. Instead let go and allow your thoughts to wallow in sexual fantasies. Suppressed sex is dangerous and leads to imbalance in the Swadishthana chakra.

(Pause for 20 seconds)

This chakra is orange in color. It is important for you to now visual the orange color expand into other aspects of your life, the creative side.

Now, flip your sexual imagery into creative energy. Feel the creative energy blossom. Nurture the feeling.

(Pause for 20 seconds)

Now it is time to make a vow. From now onward, whenever you start having sexual fantasies you will no longer negate the feelings. You will go through the experience and then when you are done with the vivid imagery, you will flip the imagery into creative pursuits.

Balancing the Swadishthana chakra means balancing your sexual and your creative urges. Over a period of time, the Swadishthana chakra will be completely awakened and blossom like a lotus flower.

Now, bring your focus to your navel area. Your navel or stomach region is represented by fire. This is called Manipura or the place of jewels. An unbalanced Manipura chakra results in low self-esteem. Many emotions are connected to your stomach. Your stomach contracts when you feel fear. The pit of the stomach also responds to jealousy.

This leads to erosion in your self-confidence. You are suspicious and display a lack of faith in others. The fire burns eternally in your Manipur chakra. Now, bring to your mind all the negative emotions you have experienced in the past one day. Explore the feeling.

Sensual Rituals

Creating Sacred Spaces for Sensual Exploration and Self-Discovery

Sensual rituals provide a sacred container for deepening your connection with your senses and exploring the realms of pleasure, self-discovery, and spiritual growth. These rituals invite you to create intentional spaces where you can fully immerse yourself in the exploration of your sensuality. Here are some suggestions for creating sensual rituals:

1. Create a Sacred Altar:

   - Set up a dedicated space in your home as a sacred altar for your sensual rituals. Decorate it with meaningful objects, candles, flowers, or symbolic representations of sensuality and divinity.

- Use your altar as a focal point for intention-setting, meditation, or simply as a reminder to honor your senses and embrace your sensual self.

2. Sensory Meditations:

- Set aside time for sensory-focused meditations. Sit in a comfortable position, close your eyes, and bring your attention to each of your senses, one at a time. Explore the sensations, images, memories, and emotions that arise as you engage with each sense.

3. Sensual Explorations:

- Designate specific times or occasions for sensual explorations. Create an ambiance that supports relaxation and pleasure, such as dim lighting, soft music, or aromatic scents.

- Engage in activities that invite sensual experiences, such as tasting a variety of foods mindfully, experimenting with different textures during a self-massage, or indulging in a sensory journey through touch, taste, smell, and sound.

4. Journaling and Reflection:

- Keep a sensual journal where you can document your experiences, thoughts, and reflections on your sensual explorations. Use this as a tool for self-discovery, personal growth, and tracking your sensual evolution.

Through these sensual rituals, you create intentional spaces where you can fully immerse yourself in the exploration of your senses. They become invitations to deepen your connection with your sensual self, awaken your erotic nature, and cultivate a profound sense of presence and pleasure.

By embracing sensuality, honoring your body, and engaging in sensual rituals, you embark on a transformative journey of self-discovery, connection, and spiritual growth. These practices allow you to cultivate a deep connection with your senses, awakening the dormant power of your erotic self and expanding your capacity for pleasure, joy, and fulfillment.

As you explore sensory awareness, engage with sight, touch, taste, smell, and sound, you open yourself to the richness and beauty of the present moment. By immersing yourself in the sensory tapestry of life, you heighten your experiences, deepen your appreciation for the world around you, and nurture a profound sense of gratitude for the gift of your senses.

By honoring your body, embracing self-care, body positivity, and self-love, you create a loving relationship with yourself and your physical form. This fosters a sense of acceptance, confidence, and empowerment, allowing you to fully embrace your sensual nature and honor the unique beauty of your body.

Through sensual rituals, you carve out sacred spaces for self-exploration and self-discovery. These intentional practices invite you to delve into the depths of your desires, emotions, and sensations, creating an opportunity for profound transformation and connection with your authentic self. By engaging in sensual rituals, you cultivate a deeper understanding of your sensual preferences, awaken your innate sensuality, and nourish your soul with the richness of pleasure and self-expression.

Imagine the possibilities that arise when you embrace sensuality as a path to spiritual growth. You unlock the potential to live a life infused with joy, passion, and deep connection. By fully embracing your senses and honoring your body, you tap into a wellspring of personal power and creative energy that can be channeled into all areas of your life.

As you embark on this journey of awakening the erotic self, I invite you to approach each moment with curiosity, openness, and a willingness to explore the depths of your sensuality. Embrace the beauty of sensory awareness, honor the wisdom of your body, and create sacred spaces for sensual rituals. In doing so, you invite a profound transformation that radiates from within, touching every aspect of your being and opening you up to a world of pleasure, self-discovery, and spiritual growth.

Embrace the sensuality that lies dormant within you. Awaken the erotic self and embark on a journey of profound self-connection, pleasure, and spiritual expansion. The path of sensuality is a gateway to the depths of your being, a portal to self-discovery and ecstatic living. Embrace it fully, and let your senses guide you towards the fulfillment and liberation that awaits.

REASON FOR DETERIORATION OF BALANCE OF THE SPEAK CHAKRA.

The one who commands the Speak Chakra is the Soul Chakra. The Speak Chakra only obeys orders. When one sees poverty or richness according to one's own achievements in the material world, then we consider it to be true and also feel and experience it. But it is not the reality. So, believing that unreal experience, that feeling as truth; the Soul Chakra makes it its firm belief. According to the same wrong belief, the Soul Chakra keeps on giving wrong commands to its Speak Chakra to take its life in the wrong direction. According to the same order, the Speak Chakra controls all the Chakras below it.

Let us take some real-life examples:

Assume that, if a person does not get proper respect in someone's home, then he feels low and while evaluating himself, considers himself inferior to others. And then he becomes so serious about this thing that he always tries to prove himself and show that he is the best. But the feeling of inferiority is constantly inside him due to which his mental balance always remains disturbed. Because of this all his Chakras become unbalanced. Because of this inferiority complex, the thyroid gland releases such hormones through the speech cycle, which have a very bad effect on the body as well as the mind.

He always feels like eating a lot. He cannot control this desire to eat. This is called hypothyroidism in medical language. This is the reason for obesity and excessive weight gain in the body. Obesity itself gives birth too many other diseases.

This shows that without controlling our own Chakras (Mind), we give our control to others. When we measure our worth by what others say, it means that we are not in control of ourselves; we are under the control of others. If someone says bad things about us, we feel bad and if the same person speaks well about us, we feel good. And then we always try to behave in such a way that, others like it. This makes us a people pleasing person. In such a situation, whatever work we do, we face humiliation, everyone demeans us.

Because we are doing it for others not for ourselves, our mind can never be stable and happy. And nothing can be done properly with an unsteady, unhappy mind. We don't know who is controlling our mind and how to keep our mind happy. But that bad experience repeatedly makes us feel inferior in our own eyes. This is what is the main reason for the deterioration of the Speak Chakra.

This type of situation is observed in many families, where in some homes women are looked down upon in the family. While it is the woman who takes care of the whole family but no one respects her. Everyone has to stay under the pressure of the elder of the house.

In such a situation, those women look down upon themselves as inferior, because they don't know how to overcome the problem. This is the reason that their thyroid gland becomes inactive. Because of which most of the women begin to live in a lot of tension and worry. And because of this, these women start eating more food, and gain more weight. Further, this obesity causes other diseases like high/low BP, diabetes, heart attack etc.

The Sacral Chakra: Law of Least Effort

The Law of Least Effort means you must accept the things you can't change, quit fighting what is happening, and stop feeling worried and anxious about the future. Life is unpredictable, and trying to control the outcome forces your way against what the universe is crafting for you.

These are the main principles governing this law:

Acceptance

As explained, the law requires that you accept what is happening for the highest good. This doesn't mean you just sit and do nothing. It means to do what feels right. If that means going to see a doctor or going to a yoga class or meditating, then you go ahead and do it. Your body energy is always your best guide. Acceptance means that when a bad situation happens, such as a relationship breakup, you don't dwell on negative thoughts. Instead, you accept the event, use the lessons learned from that experience, believe it's for your highest good, and move forward trusting that better things lie ahead.

Take Responsibility

The Law of Least Effort also means to take responsibility for your own life by taking real action to move ahead toward what you want. Taking responsibility helps you feel secure and joyful that you have what it takes to go forward, despite the size of the step. It helps move your energy within the sacral center to creation. It also means seeing the part you played in a situation (a break-up, for example) and owning those actions.

Surrender

Surrendering can be the hardest thing, because we need control. However, when you let go and move with the flow, you allow the energy within you to flow just like a river, surrendering by looking for the path that allows flow with the least effort.

When you allow the sacral energy to move freely into higher energy centers, it fuels the creative energy that enables you to compose a beautiful song, for example, look for options to bring wellness if you are feeling disease, write a book, or create a life of your dreams.

Every problem you encounter has another side: a solution from your creative energy found in your sacral center. It's so powerful that when two people come together with this energy, a human being is created. This energy can be used to create anything, provided you believe it's possible, you have faith (trust) in this energy, and you are doing it for good. This energy can be harnessed for unimaginable things. When you use it for good, it can create well-being within you and in others, too.

Restoring balance in this chakra creates an empowered and confident individual. When this chakra is balanced, you flow gracefully with life and can experience desire and pleasure. It also helps you build strong relationships and creates deep intimacy with life itself. Your creative and sexual energies flow easily and with grace.

3.2 Tools for Chakra Healing

Chakra healing involves working with the energy centers in our subtle body to restore balance and harmony. While chakra healing primarily relies on our intention and energy, various tools can enhance and support the healing process. In this chapter, we will explore a range of tools for chakra healing, each with its unique benefits and applications. By incorporating these tools into your chakra healing practice, you can deepen your connection, facilitate energy flow, and experience profound healing and transformation.

Crystals and Gemstones:

Crystals and gemstones are widely used in chakra healing due to their unique energetic properties. Each crystal corresponds to specific chakras, amplifying their energy and promoting balance. Some commonly used crystals for chakra healing include:

- Clear Quartz: Known as the "Master Healer," clear quartz is versatile and can be used to amplify the energy of all chakras.
- Amethyst: Associated with the crown chakra, amethyst enhances spiritual connection and supports meditation and intuition.
- Rose Quartz: Linked to the heart chakra, rose quartz promotes love, compassion, and emotional healing.
- Citrine: Aligned with the solar plexus chakra, citrine energizes and supports

confidence, abundance, and personal power.
- Lapis Lazuli: Connected to the third eye chakra, lapis lazuli enhances intuition, inner vision, and spiritual awareness.
- Red Jasper: Associated with the root chakra, red jasper grounds and stabilizes energy, promoting a sense of security and stability.

To use crystals for chakra healing, place them on or near the corresponding chakra during meditation, energy work, or relaxation. You can also carry or wear crystals as jewelry to benefit from their energy throughout the day.

MEDITATION USING THE HEART CHAKRA MANTRA "YAM"

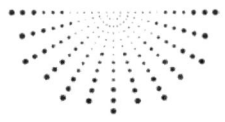

The seed (or bija in Sanskrit) mantra that corresponds with the Heart chakra is "YAM." Repeating this mantra during a Heart chakra meditation will help support concentration and focus your energy on your heart-opening intention for the meditation (to heal and balance the Heart centre, inviting love, trust, compassion and forgiveness and releasing judgement, sadness and grief).

You can chant out loud, whisper or even repeat mantras in your mind, but it is always recommended to chant the mantra out loud to create powerful vibrations through your chest and heart centre. The louder you chant and the more breath and power you put into the mantra, the stronger the vibrations you will produce. When chanting the mantra sound "YAM" during meditation, you will feel energy and vibrations in the centre of your chest, at the location of your fourth energy centre.

During a chakra mantra meditation, it's very helpful to listen to music with frequencies that can help tune and heal the specific chakra.

639 Hz is the Solfeggio frequency of the Heart - the vibration of the Heart chakra. It is known as the frequency of love and healing, connected with relationships, intimacy and vulnerability. It has the power to transform even the most fearful, angry, judgemental or heavy hearts into a heart space full of compassion, love and forgiveness. The 639 Hz frequency can help open and tune the Heart centre and can help resolve relationship problems - with family, a partner or friends. This loving frequency can also create harmonious interpersonal relationships, nurture the relationship with oneself, and enhances understanding, patience and love.

Play music in the background as you chant - you can search YouTube for a video with the Heart chakra frequency. The audiobook version of this guide will provide music with frequencies to tune the Heart chakra (they will start playing later in the chapter when you are ready to begin your meditation).

As you meditate on the Heart chakra, remember that this chakra represents the air and wind element, while the seed mantra "YAM" is connected to our control over the breath and air flow through our body. Smile at your Heart centre. Imagine your Heart space as a fresh, fragrant flower full of love, radiating this love out into the world and throughout your own mind, body and spirit. As you meditate along with the frequencies, let go of any resentment, judgement or feelings of unworthiness inside your heart. Feel it become softer, warmer and lighter.

Bring your attention to your Heart chakra. Imagine a bright green, spinning sphere of light energy in the centre of your chest. Connect to this energy. With each loud chant of "YAM," you will feel vibrations and energetic movement in your chest and Heart centre, moving down your arms - focus on this feeling. As always, feel free to experiment with different paces and volumes that feel the best for you.

Allow your Heart chakra to expand and glow brighter with every inhale, and spread its green light energy throughout your body on every exhale. With each breath, let go of fear and judgement and invite love and compassion into your Heart space.

Close your eyes and continue chanting, paying attention to your breath and Heart chakra.

The Second Chakra — Svadhisthana

The second chakra is also often called the sacral chakra. Its Sanskrit name means "sweetness." It is the element of Water. It is the place of emotion and sexuality. It is the right "To Feel." This is the place of pleasure, fluid movement, creativity, and passion.

This chakra is associated with the color orange and is located in the area just below the navel in your lower abdomen and is associated with the bladder, female reproductive organs, lymphatic system, and pelvis. It is connected to the sense of taste.

When your sacral chakra is balanced, you will feel happy, joyful, creative, passionate, and capable of connecting physically. This is also where the drive to procreate exists.

When your sacral chakra is imbalanced, you may feel unworthy, isolated, numb, stiff, overly sensitive, and emotional. You may also have a sexual addiction, or what is called sexual anorexia, hormone imbalance, and potential for miscarriages or difficulty conceiving.

This is a place where you block your emotions. Here is where you can restrict the flow of energy as a whole. It is important to do the emotional work necessary, recovering lost feelings and sometimes re-experiencing them so that you can heal and release them as you continue your awakening journey. Ultimately, when you heal and unblock your sacral chakra, you can allow a healthy flow of your emotional energy so you can experience pleasure through body movement and sexuality. Unblocking your sacral chakra can allow you to experience change, growth, and connection with your passionate self.

The Third Chakra — Manipura

The third chakra is also known as the solar plexus chakra. Its Sanskrit name means "lustrous gem." It is the element of Fire. It is power, and it is energy. It is the right "To Act." This is the place of personal power, the strength of will, and the sense of purpose.

This chakra is associated with the color yellow, and it is located between the area just below the navel and the base of the sternum. The physical feature associated with the solar chakra is the adrenal glands. Your adrenal glands regulate metabolism, blood pressure, and your immune system.

When the chakra is in balance, you will feel energy and drive, confidence, a sense of respect for others, as well as respect for the self, an active and cheerful disposition, and a strong sense of purpose.

An imbalance of the solar plexus chakra can represent as an arrogant demeanor, demanding attitude, overbearing sensibilities, and addictions. The opposite side of imbalance would look like a deficiency of energy, helplessness, a feeling of weakness, timidity, and a submissive life approach.

This chakra demonstrates a significant turning point in Kundalini awakening. It will cause a profound shift in your intentions, intuitions, self-value, and ability to see the beauty in the world. This is where judgment, biases, and prejudice melt away, first with the self and then the whole world around you. This is where you begin to feel your Kundalini power, but there is still so much more to go through.

6. TheChakras Functionality

Welcome to "Awakening Energy: Understanding Our Chakras." In this ebook, we will explore the fascinating world of chakras and their profound impact on our physical, emotional, and spiritual well-being. Together, we will delve into the functionality of the seven major chakras, unraveling their secrets and discovering practical ways to balance and harmonize these energy centers for optimal vitality and transformation. In short, CHAKRA means energy centers which are imaginary in nature around 4 – 5 inches in diameter for a normal human being.

1: The Root Chakra -

Foundation and Stability

Learn about the foundational energy center, the Root Chakra. Discover how it governs our sense of safety, security, and grounding. Explore techniques to strengthen this chakra, enhance feelings of stability, and manifest abundance in the physical realm.

2: The Sacral Chakra -

Creativity and Passion
Dive into the realm of the Sacral Chakra, the center of creativity and passion. Uncover its influence on our

emotions, sensuality, and ability to experience joy. Explore practices to balance this chakra, unleash your creative potential, and cultivate healthy relationships.

3: The Solar Plexus Chakra - Personal Power and Confidence

Explore the Solar Plexus Chakra, the seat of personal power and confidence. Understand its role in self-

esteem, willpower, and manifestation. Learn techniques to activate and balance this chakra, empowering you to step into your authentic power and achieve your goals.

4: The Heart Chakra - Love and Compassion

Open your heart to the transformative energy of the Heart Chakra. Discover its significance in

experiencing love, compassion, and connection with ourselves and others. Embrace practices to heal and harmonize this chakra, allowing love to flow freely in your life.

5: The Throat Chakra - Communication and Expression

Unleash the power of your voice through the Throat Chakra. Explore how it influences our ability to express ourselves authentically and communicate effectively. Learn techniques to balance this chakra, speak your truth, and express your unique creative expression.

6: The Third Eye Chakra -

Intuition and Inner Wisdom
Tap into the realm of intuition and higher knowledge with

the Third Eye Chakra. Discover how it enhances our perception, insight, and spiritual connection. Dive into practices to awaken and balance this chakra, expanding your consciousness and accessing your inner wisdom.

7: The Crown Chakra - Unity and Spiritual Awakening

Experience the divine energy of the Crown Chakra, our gateway to spiritual connection and enlightenment. Explore its influence on our consciousness, higher states of awareness, and divine guidance. Engage in practices to open and align this chakra, experiencing profound spiritual awakening and unity.

Congratulations on expanding your knowledge of the seven major chakras. By understanding their functionality and engaging in practices to balance and harmonize these energy centers, you are embarking on a transformative journey of self-discovery and spiritual growth. Embrace the wisdom and power within your chakras and unlock the limitless potential that awaits you.

Effective Chanting Techniques:

Effective chanting goes beyond good pronunciation and covers numerous ways to optimize the transforming power of mantras. Here are some fundamental chanting techniques:

1. Breath Awareness: Coordinate your chanting with your breath. Inhale deeply before commencing the chant, and let the music flow freely with your expiration. This synchronization promotes the flow of prana (life energy) and maintains a constant beat.

2. Attention and Mindfulness: Maintain undivided attention on the mantra when chanting. If the mind wanders, gently bring it back to the sound of the mantra. Cultivate awareness and immerse yourself entirely in the practice.

3. Repetition and Mala: Mantras are generally rhythmically sung several times. Use a mala (prayer beads) to keep track of repetitions. Chanting a defined number of times boosts attention and intensifies the energy effect.

4. Intention and Visualization: Infuse each Repetition with your sense and imagine the mantra's meaning or heavenly embodiment. This gives depth to your practice and enhances the potency of the chant.

5. Group Chanting: Chanting mantras improve collective energy and provide a supportive and uplifting atmosphere. Group chanting may be a powerful experience, increasing the advantages of solo practice.

6. Adjusting Volume and Pace: Experiment with various volumes and paces of chanting. Some mantras are more effective when sung quietly and slowly, while others may have a more dramatic impact when chanted with passion and speed.

*7. Emotional Connectio*n: Engage your emotions in the chanting process. Feel the vibration of the mantra inside your heart. Embrace the feelings that come when chanting, allowing them to resonate with the mantra's energy.

8. Silent Chanting (AjapaJapa): Advanced practitioners may investigate the practice of "AjapaJapa," where the mantra is mentally recited quietly with the breath. This technique helps deepen meditation and strengthen the mantra's subtle influence.

9. Pause and Absorption: After finishing a cycle of chanting, take a minute to sit in quiet and absorb the energy influence of the mantra. Feel the reverberation of the music echoing inside your being.

10. Closure and thanks: After your mantra practice, say a closing prayer or express gratitude for the experience. Acknowledge the divine and the transformational power of the mantra in your life.

Chakras and Physical Health

The chakras affect our emotional and spiritual well-being and are crucial to our physical health. Each chakra is associated with specific physical parts of the body, and blockages or imbalances in these chakras can lead to physical symptoms and illness. This chapter will explore the relationship between the chakras and physical health and how chakra healing can promote physical healing and well-being.

The Chakras and Physical Health

Each chakra is associated with specific physical parts of the body, and imbalances or blockages in these chakras can lead to physical symptoms and illness. Here are some examples:

> The root chakra is associated with the legs, feet, and lower body. An imbalanced root chakra

can lead to constipation, lower back pain, and leg and foot problems.

The sacral chakra is associated with the reproductive organs, bladder, and lower intestines. An imbalanced sacral chakra can lead to menstrual problems, urinary tract infections, and sexual dysfunction.

The solar plexus chakra is associated with the digestive system, liver, and gallbladder. An imbalanced solar plexus chakra can lead to indigestion, ulcers, and liver problems.

The heart chakra is associated with the heart, lungs, and circulatory system. An imbalanced heart chakra can lead to high blood pressure, heart disease, and respiratory problems.

The throat chakra is associated with the throat, neck, and jaw. An imbalanced throat chakra can lead to sore throat, thyroid problems, and jaw pain.

The third eye chakra is associated with the brain, nervous system, and eyes. An imbalanced third eye chakra can lead to migraines, vision problems, and neurological disorders.

The crown chakra is associated with the brain and the entire body. An imbalanced crown chakra can lead to headaches, insomnia, and chronic fatigue.

Chakra Healing for Physical Health

Chakra healing can be a powerful tool for promoting physical healing and well-being. By balancing and activating the chakras, we can remove blockages and promote the free flow of energy throughout the body. Here are some ways to use chakra healing for physical health:

Chakra meditation: By meditating on each chakra, we can bring awareness to any imbalances or blockages and work to balance and activate them.

Chakra yoga: Practicing yoga poses that focus on specific

chakras can help to open and balance those chakras.

Chakra crystals: Placing crystals on the specific chakras can help to remove blockages and balance the energy flow.

- Chakra sound therapy: Listening to specific sound frequencies can help to activate and balance the chakras.

Throat-Opening Exercises

You may or may not have noticed that the energy-opening exercises we've included in the previous chapters revolve around physically expanding and opening the parts of the body where the imbalanced or closed Chakra is located. Opening our Heart requires us to expand our chest cavity, for example, while opening our Solar Plexus prompts us to position ourselves in a way that requires the utmost bodily control. The following Throat-opening exercises are no exception: they encourage us to engage our throats in physical actions that open and clear them so that the Chakra located within may be cleared and balanced as well.

- **Gurgling:** Although it's a rather simple exercise—simply fill your mouth with water, tilt your head back, and gurgle (making sure to push the water as far back as possible), gurgling can have rather therapeutic effects on our throats. If you have a sore throat—a symptom of a closed Throat—for instance, you'll want to gurgle with salt water. This will ease your sore throat while simultaneously opening your Throat Chakra.

- **Yelling:** Again, a rather simple exercise, but an effective one nonetheless. A closed

Throat limits our ability to communicate and restrains our self-expression. Yet, when we yell, we force our throats to make noise. The way we yell—the pitch and the length of time we do it for—lets use express ourselves even if we're unable to do it verbally. The aggressive outburst of noise that comes from our throat when we yell helps clear any energy-restricting barriers that have formed in our throats.

- **Plow pose:** This meditative posture is one

that will help you become more aware of your Throat and its location in your body. Sometimes, all an imbalanced Chakra needs is an acknowledgement of its presence and a little physical attention. Plow pose does just this:

1.) Lie on your back with your arms fully extended (but relaxed) by your side. They should be parallel with the rest of your body. Your head should rest normal, face turned toward the ceiling.

2.) With your palms turned face down, lift your legs above your head. Keep rotating your legs back until your toes touch the ground *behind* your head. Let you down-turned palms and toes balance you.

3.) While you remain in this position for 1 minute, notice any sensations you experience in your neck. Consider: *Do my neck and throat feel constricted in any way? Do I notice my throat's presence in this position more than I normally do?*

Potential Causes of Interference with the Root Chakra

If someone says that they are trying to fix a troubled root chakra they usually means that they are attempting to open up constricted pathways of energy that are causing deficiency. But in some cases, the pathways aren't blocked, but rather, they are simply overused. The first step of fixing an imbalanced root chakra is to ascertain whether the chakra is deficient or overactive. Fortunately for us, there are some pretty easy to follow cues that aid in this determination.

If a person is excessively sluggish, for example, with a distinct lack of energy, that person is most likely suffering from a deficient chakra. If on the other hand, someone is hyper, constantly in a state of agitation, and excessively vigilant, they just might have an overactive chakra. Those with an overactive chakra will also exhibit traits such as flashes of anger, excessive round-the-clock work, and even instances of hoarding. In the end, all of this behavior is due to a deep sense of insecurity.

Here are some direct causes of interference with the root chakra:

- Being Disorganized

There is an expression: "A disorganized home is the cause of a disorganized mind." You can also say that a disorganized home is the cause of a disorganized root chakra! Because it's very true that having a disorganized living space, work place, or even just a disordered weekly schedule can have direct impact upon your root chakra. As you can see, if you would like to restore your root chakra, cleaning your house might actually be a good start. But this effort of organization is more than straightening up your home and office – it also comes down to straightening up your goals and priorities in life. If you feel like you are becoming disconnected from your root chakra you just might want to do a self-evaluation, and figure out exactly what is important to you in life, and how you can work toward pursuing those goals.

- Becoming Alienated

It may seem like a bit of a redundancy, but if you are feeling the alienating symptoms of a busted root chakra, it just might be because you have become alienated. You see, some forms of alienation are not always within our control and can catch us off guard, breaking through all of our defenses. Environmental factors often come into play with this. If someone is in a situation or environment in which they constantly feel at odds with those around them, this can lead to significant damage to their root chakra. Ultimately, feelings of alienation stem from feeling unaccepted by either your immediate friends and family or society at large. One needs to take a proactive stance of unity and love in order to prevent such an experience. If you feel that you are indeed becoming alienated from your peers or society at large, you should find ways to participate in social gatherings. Whether you join a church, a volunteer group, or a social club, make sure that you find a way to put yourself around a group of good people to become connected with.

- Money Trouble

In modern human society, money is inescapably interwoven with our security and sense of well-being. It is, therefore, not surprising that trouble with finances can lead to the insecurity felt by a disrupted root chakra. Interestingly enough, the converse is true as well, and it could be a lack of self-worth and "rootedness" that can cause issues with money in the first place. Either way, money trouble can most certainly be attributed to a faulty root chakra. When the energy is not flowing through your root chakra the right way, it could lead to disruptions in your checkbook through bad financial decisions. So, if finances are giving you grief, you just might want to get to the root of the issue by taking a look at the state of your root chakra.

- Chronic Illness

In some cases, chronic physical ailments, especially those connected to the immune system, can cause the development of blockages in your root chakra. In such instances, the person is slowly worn down by a very real threat to their physical condition. And since the root chakra is our sense of stability in the physical world, it is only natural for it to begin to waver and shut down, just as the physical body begins to do so. If this chakra is disrupted, chronic illness could be a result.

- Troubled Relationships

Being in troubled personal relationships can, after a time, take a toll on your root chakra and have you questioning your core beliefs, doubting who you even are. If no other reason can be ascertained as to why a root chakra is blocked, troubled relationships could be a contributing factor. Sometimes, you just need to make an evaluation of those around you and try to determine just what it is you are getting out of the relationship.

How Can We Diagnose a Chakra Imbalance?

Chakras are the spinning circles of our energy system, pulling energy in that needs to be renewed and transmitting healthier energy outwards once again. They are located vertically along the center line of the body, over the spine. Each one is associated with an endocrine center of the body and so regulates the flow of hormones, energy, and stimulation in that area.

If they stop to work correctly and become blocked or imbalanced, then they will either pull in too much energy or even cease to work completely. This has a knock-on effect on the rest of the other chakras, and so secondary and associated systems can occur.

If we have problems in any of the following areas of the body where the chakras are located, then we can immediately presume chakra imbalance:

- Root troubles: IBS; stomach upset; and difficulty in sitting, sleeping, or lying down

- Sacral troubles: sexual health, digestion, and fertility problems

- Solar plexus troubles: sense of unease, low self-worth, and anxiety

- Heart troubles: arrhythmia; low or high blood pressure; sadness; and unable to feel dynamic, energized, or happy

- Throat troubles: problem in breathing, coughs, difficulty in talking, colds, and sinus problems.

- Third eye troubles: insight, vision, and eyesight problems and paranoia

- Crown chakra troubles: thinking problems, foggy minded, and daydreaming

Assessing Chakra Health

Luckily, as well as assessing ourselves using the above list of symptoms, there is also a very easy way to diagnose chakra imbalances.

You will need only

- a pendulum

Using a crystal, stone, or favorite dowsing object on some thin twine, you can hold the pendulum over each chakra and 'ask' for its size, speed, and direction. Using this simple method, you can assess each one to see if some are spinning fast or too slow and are over large or too small.

Place the pendulum over each chakra, asking your questions as to its condition and state, and try to detect whether you feel any residue of heat, cold, unease, or sickness.

You can also use the same technique to ask which stone, crystal, color, or medicine to use for each chakra, by holding the pendulum over each and asking for the results!

Chapter 2: What Blocks a Chakra?

Now that you're familiar with what chakras are, you may be wondering what causes a blockage in your chakras, and thus prevents it from functioning properly. A blocked chakra may be the result of a number of things, and can leave you feeling sick or unhealthy both physically and emotionally, and just flat-out drained.

People with blocked chakras can often feel like a passenger sitting in the backseat of their own car, unable to have any sense of control over what happens on the road - or in their case, what happens in their life. This feeling is characterized by the loss of control in your life.

Here are some of the causes that lead to a blocked and weakened chakra:

Childhood traumas, physical and emotional injuries, having a limited belief system, cultural conditioning, and bad habits can all cause a blockage in the energy flowing through your chakras, often resulting in physical and emotional low-vitality. Fear, anxiety and stress are all very common causes of imbalanced and weakened chakras.

Does it seem like your financial situation, personal relationships, or physical and emotional health have been falling apart and going down the drain, leading you to suffer even more stress, anxiety and frustration? If so, you can improve all of these aspects in your life by improving and rebalancing your chakras! Although it sounds so simple, and even too good to be true, improving the flow of energy to your 7 energy centers, or chakras will leave you feeling much healthier, both physically and emotionally, as well as immensely improve your overall well-being.

Energy centers that are depleted of energy = lack of energy and well being. It's that simple.

Going back to the "passenger in your own car" example that was mentioned above - by rebalancing your chakras and improving the flow of energy throughout your body, you will easily be able to grab the steering wheel and regain control over your life!

CHAPTER TWO

ABOUT YOGA

Yoga is a practice of well-being and relaxation based on the liberation of chakras to resolve psychophysical tensions. We reveal the beneficial effects of yoga on both physical and mental fitness. Benefits, dangers, rates, different types of yoga

THE ORIGINS OF YOGA

Yoga is increasingly practiced more often for its physical benefits than for its benefits on the mind, yet both are related and the physical and mental state are improved at the same time after a few months of regular practice.

Some famous doctors see in Yoga a precious help to the prevention against certain chronic diseases. Yoga is a discipline aimed, through meditation, asceticism moral and physical exercises, to achieve the unification of the human being in its physical, mental and spiritual.

Yoga does not exclude the metaphysical plane of the physical plane and the mental plane. He does not separate matter from thought.

His method encompasses all knowledge, the structure of the apparent world, the formation of thought, the role of the energy that gives rise to the one and the other, and, beyond that, the energetic and creative power of which the world is born. By the method of reintegration, it allows to perceive the nature of the mental representations and the conscience and to arrive at the union with the subtle form of the being.

Yoga is one of the six schools (ṣaḍdarśana) of Vedic philosophy. The word "yoga" comes from Sanskrit, meaning is much broader than the commonly given definition of "union".

Its Sanskrit root yuj means "harness, unite".

The word "yoga" has, in Sanskrit, the following meanings:

1) Hitching action;

2) Method of training horses;

3) Instructions for use, technique;

4) Spiritual discipline;

5) raja-yoga;

6) hatha-yoga;

7) State of union or unity of the subjective being with the Supreme.

So we see that yoga is the method, the means, and the goal.

Hatha Yoga

For a majority of Westerners, yoga comes down to Hatha Yoga. Yet not only is it not the only form of yoga, but even the form proposed in the West is far removed from what traditional Hatha Yoga is.

Indeed, Hatha-Yoga, traditionally, is not a form of gentle gymnastics but a spiritual path in its own right, moreover a steep and dangerous path reserved for an elite of individuals ready to burn the stages of Realization.

The term "haṭha" means force, violence. From a symbolic point of view, it also expresses the happy meeting of opposites, found in the praṇava, the sacred syllable om (the lunar crescent hosting the solar point).

From a technical point of view, Hatha-Yoga is a discipline of harmonization and development of the psychological (concentration, serenity) and bodily (power and flexibility) faculties pushed to their perfection.

The term yoga means "union" in Sanskrit. This ancestral practice originating in India preaches the union of the body and the spirit and the union of the individual soul (ours) and the universal soul (the Creator). This practice was originally transmitted from teacher to student.

www.ingramcontent.com/pod-product-compliance
Lightning Source LLC
Chambersburg PA
CBHW052143110526
44591CB00012B/1843